MW01517130

The Ryan Reynolds Story

An Intimate Portrait of the Actor, Producer, and Comic Genius

By Jean Winchester

THE RYAN REYNOLDS STORY

An Intimate Portrait of the Actor, Producer, and Comic Genius

BY

JEAN WINCHESTER

All rights reserved. No part of this publication may be reproduced, distributed, or transmitted in any form or by any means, including photocopying, recording, or other electronic or mechanical methods, without the prior written permission of the copyright owner, except in the case of brief quotations embodied in critical reviews and certain other noncommercial uses permitted by copyright law.

Copyright © Jean Winchester, 2024.

TABLE OF CONTENTS

INTRODUCTION

Welcome, dear Readers, to the enchanting excursion through the life and tradition of a Hollywood illuminator — Ryan Reynolds. In the accompanying pages, we leave on an investigation of the complex profession of an entertainer, maker, business visionary, and altruist whose story reaches out a long way past the glinting lights of the cinema.

From the early parts that unwind the difficulties of his early stages to the climactic minutes that pushed him to the pinnacle of Hollywood fame, this book tries to lay out an extensive representation of Reynolds' momentous vocation. Together, we will explore the exciting bends in the road of a story that traverses kinds, resists shows, and makes a permanent imprint on media outlets.

Lock in as we dig into the background stories of leading-edge jobs, the groundbreaking excursion of becoming Deadpool, and Reynolds' introduction to the domains of creation and business venture. In any case, the story doesn't stop there — it stretches out into the core of altruism, uncovering what makes Reynolds' heart and the effect he endeavors to make past the reel.

As we turn the pages, we welcome you to observe not just the ups and downs of a Hollywood symbol yet in addition the certified energy, strength, and realness that characterize Ryan Reynolds. This is more than a memoir; it's an excursion through the layers of a social character peculiarity — one clever comment, one historic job, and each magnanimous demonstration in turn.

In this way, go along with us as we disentangle the parts of a daily existence that go past the prearranged lines, uncovering a heritage that reverberates with the powerful soul of a left a permanent man engraved on the material of diversion and then some. Welcome to the spellbinding universe of Ryan Reynolds.

CHAPTER 1

Background and Early Life

Young Reynolds

Ryan Rodney Reynolds was brought into the world on October 23, 1976, in Vancouver, English Columbia, Canada. Experiencing childhood in an unassuming family, Reynolds displayed early indications of his future magnetic character. His dad, Jim Reynolds, functioned as a food distributor, while his mom, Tammy, held different positions, including retail deals.

During his early stages, Reynolds went to Kitsilano Auxiliary School, where he displayed an early interest in acting. Notwithstanding his normal ability, he at first sought an alternate way, selecting Kwantlen Polytechnic College to concentrate on acting. Be that as it may, his actual enthusiasm drove him to nonconformist and spotlight on seeking an acting profession.

Reynolds' excursion to Hollywood began with TV jobs in the mid-1990s. He acquired consideration for his work on shows like "**Hillside**" and "**Two Guys and a Girl**," laying the preparation for his future achievement. This period was set apart by tirelessness and commitment as he sharpened his specialty, planning for the valuable open doors that would ultimately move him into the spotlight.

The change from the Canadian diversion scene to Hollywood was not without its difficulties. Despite early difficulties and a progression of jobs that didn't earn boundless respect, Reynolds stayed versatile. His assurance paid off when he landed advancement jobs that would make way for his ascent to fame.

The early long stretches of Ryan Reynolds' life molded his profession as well as established the groundwork for the sensible character that would make him a cherished figure in media outlets. His Canadian roots and early battles are basic pieces of the account that characterize the man behind the magnetic exhibitions on screen.

Setting the Stage: Canada to Hollywood

Ryan Reynolds' excursion from his Canadian roots to the style and fabulousness of Hollywood is a story wealthy in assurance and desire. After acquiring beginning involvement with Canadian TV, Reynolds put his focus on the bigger phase of Hollywood, where dreams are both fashioned and tried.

In the last part of the '90s, Reynolds settled on the essential choice to move to Los Angeles, denoting a critical act of pure trust in the quest for his acting desires. The progress from the Canadian media outlet to the profoundly serious scene of Hollywood was not consistent. It requested flexibility and versatility, characteristics that would become signs of Reynolds' vocation.

After showing up in Hollywood, Reynolds confronted the difficulties that many hopeful entertainers experience — tryouts that prompted the two victories and dissatisfactions. Notwithstanding early difficulties, his ability and allure steadily grabbed the eye of projecting chiefs and industry insiders. This time of steadiness and difficult work laid the preparation for what might turn into a surprising vocation.

Reynolds' most memorable remarkable advancement accompanied the 2002 satire film "**Van Wilder: Party Liaison**," where he exhibited his comedic ability. This noticeable defining moment moved him into the spotlight and opened ways to additional huge doors in the business.

The excursion from his Canadian starting points to Hollywood molded Reynolds as an entertainer as well as affected the jobs he would pick from now on. The social shift joined with the assorted encounters en route, added to the special point of view he brings to his exhibitions.

This stage in Reynolds' life fills in as a demonstration of the perseverance expected to explore the cutthroat scene of Hollywood. A part of his story features the mental fortitude to seek after one's fantasies and the groundbreaking force of facing challenges to chase imaginative satisfaction.

The Ryan Reynolds Story

14

CHAPTER 2

Rise to Stardom

Ryan Reynolds' rise to fame is a story of constancy, key decisions, and evident ability. After taking the jump from Canada to Hollywood, Reynolds confronted a progression of jobs that, while displaying his capacities, didn't quickly sling him into the notch. In any case, his assurance and obligation to his art at last made ready for cutting-edge minutes.

One of the significant achievements in Reynolds' ascent was his job in the 2002 satire "**Van Wilder: Party Liaison**." Depicting the enchanting and clever Van More out of control, Reynolds exhibited his comedic pizazz and approachable on-screen presence. The film turned into a faction exemplary and checked Reynolds as an entertainer with driving man potential.

Following "**Van Wilder**," Reynolds explored the scene of lighthearted comedies, including eminent movies like "**Definitely, Maybe**" and "**The Proposal**." His charming exhibitions and capacity to mix humor with certified feeling charmed him to crowds, setting his status as a bankable driving man.

Be that as it may, the genuine advancement accompanied the depiction of the contemptuous wannabe Deadpool in the 2016 film of a similar name. The job displayed Reynolds' comedic gifts as well as his capacity to exemplify complex characters. "**Deadpool**" was an enormous achievement, breaking film industry records for an adults-only film and procuring Reynolds far and wide recognition.

Reynolds' ascent to fame wasn't exclusively characterized by blockbuster victories. He decisively differentiated his jobs, flawlessly progressing between types. This flexibility was obvious in his exhibitions in films like "**Buried**," a strained spine chiller, and "**The Voices**," a dim satire. Such decisions showed his obligation to test himself as an entertainer and abstain from pigeonholing.

All through his excursion to fame, Reynolds kept an engaging and sensible public persona. His collaborations with fans via web-based entertainment, combined with his humble humor, charmed him to a wide crowd past the bounds of the cinema.

The ascent to fame Ryan Reynolds was not a short-term peculiarity but rather a continuous trip set apart by flexibility, vital choices, and a certified association with crowds. His process fills in as motivation for hopeful entertainers and a demonstration of the groundbreaking force of diligence in the cutthroat domain of Hollywood.

Breakthrough Roles

Ryan Reynolds' way to fame was accentuated by a progression of cutting-edge jobs that exhibited his flexibility as an entertainer and hardened his presence in media outlets.

➤ "Van Wilder: Party Liaison" (2002):

In this school satire, Reynolds depicted the appealing and easygoing Van Wilder stunning. The film, albeit at first remaining unnoticed, acquired a religious following, driving Reynolds into the spotlight and laying him out as a main man with comedic slashes.

➤ "Definitely, Maybe" (2008):

Withdrawing from the comedic domain, Reynolds assumed the job of a dad describing his heartfelt history to his girl. The film displayed his capacity to explore genuine and close-to-home stories, expanding his allure past parody.

➤ "The Proposal" (2009):

Matched opposite Sandra Bullock, Reynolds featured in this lighthearted comedy as her partner. The film's prosperity further raised Reynolds' status in the business, exhibiting his science with Top-notch co-stars and supporting his driving man qualifications.

➤ "Buried" (2010):

A takeoff from standard jobs, Reynolds featured in this spine chiller as a man covered alive. The film, set as a rule in a casket, featured his capacity to convey a strained and claustrophobic story, procuring basic recognition for his serious and singular exhibition.

➤ "Deadpool" (2016):

Seemingly the most groundbreaking job of his profession, Reynolds encapsulated the disrespectful and joking wannabe, Deadpool. The film's exceptional achievement, both basically and financially, broke assumptions for adults-only hero motion pictures. Reynolds' obligation to the job and his on-point mix of humor and activity set his place as a Hollywood Superstar.

➤ "Detective Pikachu" (2019):

Reynolds loaned his voice to the darling Pokémon character Pikachu in this true-to-life/CGI cross-breed film. The family-accommodating experience displayed Reynolds' capacity to interface with different crowds, further growing his allure past unambiguous classifications.

These advanced jobs on the whole molded Reynolds' direction in the business. From comedies to spine chillers, and superheroes to family-accommodating admission, Reynolds demonstrated his reach as an entertainer. His essential decisions and capacity to imbue humor and heart into characters added to his status as perhaps one of Hollywood's most pursued and cherished driving men.

Navigating the Challenges of Early Fame

Ryan Reynolds' excursion through the maze of early popularity was set apart by a progression of complicated difficulties, each requiring a sensitive equilibrium of versatility, thoughtfulness, and vital independent direction.

As the spotlight heightened following the progress of **"Van Wilder: Party Liaison,"** Reynolds ended up at the convergence of taking off assumptions and the persevering investigation that goes with fame. The strain to support achievement posed a potential threat, requesting a nuanced way to deal with project choice that would exhibit his flexibility while resisting the phantom of pigeonholing.

In the beginning phases of his vocation, Reynolds went up against the inborn duality of acclaim - the inebriating charm of adulation and the basic look that takes apart every presentation. Managing both worship and analysis, he utilized input as a device for development, utilizing it to refine his art and advance as an entertainer.

The direction of acclaim frequently disturbs the fragile harmony between individual and expert life. Reynolds, exploring the requests of Hollywood, confronted the test of keeping up with significant connections amid the hurricane of his thriving profession. Finding some kind of harmony requires individual thoughtfulness as well as intense attention to the cost that acclaim can take on one's confidential life.

Public examination turned into a steady friend, and Reynolds, equipped with his brand name mind, dealt with the spotlight with validness. His capacity to interface with general society on an individual level, combined with a receptive disposition, turned into a foundation of his public picture, exploring the difficulties of popularity with beauty and humor.

In any case, a few out of every odd step on the way to fame was met with adulation. Reynolds experienced mishaps, from projects that missed the mark regarding assumptions to films that confronted basic difficulties. Facing these mistakes, he transformed them into valuable open doors for learning and development, molding a story of versatility and variation.

Reynolds' initial popularity was a fragile dance on a tightrope, a difficult exercise that necessitated him to shuffle the assumptions for an industry hungry for the following huge star while remaining consistent with his specialty and individual ethos. His capacity to explore these difficulties established the groundwork for a vocation that rises above the vaporous idea of distinction, solidifying his status as a Hollywood sturdy.

CHAPTER 3

Behind the Laughter

Digging into the layers that make the comedic virtuoso out of Ryan Reynolds uncovers a story that reaches out past the screen. His capacity to implant humor into jobs goes past simple execution; it's a demonstration of a sharp comprehension of comedic timing, an appreciation for the ridiculous, and a real love for making individuals snicker.

Reynolds' excursion into the domain of chuckling is a nuanced investigation of the comedic scene. From his initial introductions to sitcoms to his breakout job in **"Van Wilder: Party Liaison,"** he exhibited a natural talent for conveying zingers with faultless timing. The progress from situational parody to highlight films was consistent, exhibiting his flexibility and reach inside the comedic range.

What recognizes Reynolds as a comedic force isn't simply his capacity to convey lines but his ability to exemplify characters that resound with humor. Whether it's the enchanting and clever Van More stunning or the contemptuous Deadpool, Reynolds brings an interesting mix of moxy and comedic reasonableness to every job.

However, behind the giggling lies a painstakingly adjusted balance. Reynolds has amazingly woven snapshots of weakness and genuineness into his comedic exhibitions. This combination of humor with veritable inclination is a characterizing part of his work, lifting his jobs past simple comedic cartoons to characters that vibe engaging and true.

Exploring the scarce difference between humor and heart in Hollywood is no simple accomplishment, yet Reynolds has done so with artfulness. His comedic decisions are not erratic; they are the consequence of a conscious way of dealing with narrating. This deliberateness is obvious in the variety of comedic classes he has embraced, from unseemly humor to family-accommodating parody, displaying a reach that rises above the bounds of a solitary comedic style.

Past the characters he depicts, Reynolds' off-screen humor is similarly vital to his comedic personality. His drawing in and clever presence via online entertainment, combined with his humble humor in interviews, has charmed him to fans and added a layer to the account of his comedic persona.

the story behind Ryan Reynolds' chuckling is a complex investigation of comedic masterfulness. A story unfurls on the stage and screen as well as in the subtleties of timing, the validity of character depiction, and the consistent transaction of humor and heart that characterizes his getting through heritage in the realm of satire.

Balancing Humor and Heart in Hollywood

One of the distinctive elements of Ryan Reynolds' Hollywood process is his remarkable capacity to strike a sensitive harmony among humor and certifiable inclination, an equilibrium that has characterized his true-to-life inheritance as well as charmed him to crowds all over the planet.

Reynolds' ability to imbue his jobs with humor is, at this point, a very much praised feature of his acting collection. Nonetheless, what separates him is the consistent coordination of genuine minutes inside the comedic accounts. This fragile dance among chuckling and earnest inclination is a demonstration of his nuanced comprehension of narrating.

In the domain of rom-coms, exemplified by films like **"Definitely, Maybe**," and **"The Proposal**," Reynolds goes past the shallow shows of the class. Indeed, there are snickers, however, woven into the comedic embroidered artwork are snapshots of weakness and bona fide association. This capacity to inject sentiment with veritable inclination lifts his movies past the standard charge, causing them to reverberate with crowds on a more profound level.

On account of his famous depiction of Deadpool, Reynolds reclassified the hero classification by infusing contemptuous humor and breaking the fourth wall. However, underneath the quips and activity-stuffed successions lies a person wrestling with torment and disengagement. This juxtaposition of humor and profundity rejuvenated the superhuman kind as well as displayed Reynolds' obligation to permeate even the most eccentric characters with a feeling of mankind.

The science of humor and heart in Reynolds' work stretches out past individual exhibitions to the general tone of his vocation. His essential decisions in projects uncover a cognizant work to offset carefree comedies with additional genuinely full jobs, making a different collection of work that requests a wide range of crowds.

Off-screen, Reynolds' humor reaches out to his public persona, where clever virtual entertainment cooperation and humble humor add to his interesting picture. This credibility builds up the thought that, even amid the charm of Hollywood, Reynolds remains grounded and associated with the regular encounters that cause us to snicker and to feel.

the craft of adjusting humor and heart in Hollywood, as exemplified by Ryan Reynolds, is a fragile transaction that rises above kinds. It's about something beyond evoking giggling; it's a cognizant work to make stories that reverberate inwardly, making an enduring effect that stretches out a long way past the comedic minutes on screen. Reynolds' capacity to explore this mind-boggling dance has set his status as a flexible and darling figure in the realm of diversion.

CHAPTER 4

Personal Life

Ryan Reynolds, underneath the facade of Hollywood fame, uncovers a rich and nuanced individual life that adds profundity to the story of his public persona.

In issues of the heart, Reynolds' heartfelt excursion has been both examined and celebrated. His union with Scarlett Johansson denoted a high-profile association, and their ensuing separation in 2010 unfurled under the spotlight. Be that as it may, Reynolds found persevering through affection with Blake Lively. Their relationship, portrayed by a blend of protection and periodic impressions imparted to people in general, has turned into an image of enduring affection in the domain of superstar connections.

Parenthood has been an extraordinary part of Reynolds. The entertainer and Vivacious offer three girls, and Reynolds doesn't avoid sharing the delights and difficulties of nurturing. His diverting tales about the characteristics of parenthood, combined with true reflections on its significant effect, resonate with many, offering an interesting viewpoint on the crossing point of distinction and day-to-day life.

The individual story takes a piercing turn with the deficiency of Reynolds' dad, James, to Parkinson's sickness. This misfortune has turned into an impetus for Reynolds' contribution to bringing issues to light about the sickness, mirroring a profundity of character and a pledge to utilize his impact for significant causes.

Past the red carpet, Reynolds embraces leisure activities that ground him in the customary. An outside fan, he tracks down comfort in setting up camp and climbing, exhibiting an affection for nature that differentiations with the charm of Tinseltown. His quest for a pilot's permit addresses an enthusiasm for flying, uncovering a man with interests past the bounds of his on-screen jobs.

Wandering into the business domain, Reynolds co-owns Aviation American Gin, a pioneering attempt that reflects monetary venture as well as a dynamic commitment to the business. This introduction to a business venture highlights his craving to broaden and expand his impact past the entertainment world.

Reynolds' web-based presence is an expansion of his off-screen character. Via virtual entertainment, he shares diverting tales, clever editorials, and brief looks into his day-to-day routine. This computerized commitment interfaces him with fans as well as features a more unfiltered side, supporting the picture of a superstar who doesn't make too much of himself.

Fundamentally, Ryan Reynolds' own life is a story woven with affection, misfortune, chuckling, and a certifiable quest for different interests. It adds layers to the narrative of a man exploring the intricacies of popularity while holding a feeling of genuineness and appeal.

Reynolds and his family

Ryan Reynolds Off-Screen: Hobbies and Passions

Past the excitement and style of Hollywood, Ryan Reynolds' off-screen persona is enlightened by a different cluster of side interests and interests that offer a brief look into the complex person behind the big name.

An energetic outdoorsman, Reynolds tracks down comfort in the effortlessness of nature. Setting up camp and climbing, pursuits frequently connected with quietude and association with the normal world, act as an offset to the excited speed of media outlets. This affection for the outside exhibits an element of Reynolds that flourishes in the peaceful excellence outside the limits of film sets and red floor coverings.

Adding one more layer to his inclinations, Reynolds has sought after an energy for flying. Going past the common quests for a Hollywood star, he has committed time and work to procure a pilot's permit. This addresses a certifiable love for flying, an undertaking that lines up with his tendency towards challenges past the cinema. The skies become material for Reynolds, outlining his readiness to investigate new regions both in his own life and in the exacting sense.

Business has likewise turned into a critical feature of Reynolds' off-screen pursuits. His association with Aviation American Gin goes past the domain of simple venture. He effectively partakes in the advancement and development of the brand, displaying a distinct fascination with business past acting. This enterprising soul adds a layer of intricacy to his off-screen character, situating him as something other than a Hollywood entertainer.

Reynolds' funny bone, a brand name of his public persona, expands flawlessly into his off-screen life. His clever and disrespectful virtual entertainment presence gives fans a window into his everyday insights, frequently bound with humble humor and genuine reflections on different parts of life. This computerized commitment interfaces him with his crowd as well as further adapts the Hollywood star, making him agreeable and interesting.

Ryan Reynolds off-screen, with his side interests and interests, is a material painted with shades of vagueness and variety. From the quietness of the outside to the excitement of flight and the difficulties of business, his interests reverberate a longing for a balanced and satisfying life past the realistic casing. Reynolds' off-screen story is a demonstration of the lavishness that exists when one's character reaches out past the jobs played on screen.

CHAPTER 5

<u>Becoming Deadpool</u>

The transformation of Ryan Reynolds into the notorious screw-up, Deadpool, is a story that rises above the regular limits of hero depictions, set apart by tirelessness, inventive perseverance, and a profound association among entertainers and characters.

Reynolds' most memorable experience with Deadpool on the big screen was in **"X-Men Origins: Wolverine"** (2009), where he depicted Swim Wilson. In any case, the film's translation of the person didn't line up with the quintessence of Deadpool from the comic books. Notwithstanding the blended gathering, Reynolds clutched the conviction that Deadpool merited a steadfast variation, making way for an excursion that would rethink his vocation.

The defining moment accompanied the Spilled test film in 2014, a bit that exhibited Reynolds completely embracing the flippant and comedic soul of Deadpool. The predominantly certain reaction from fans energized a groundswell of help, at last prompting the greenlight for an independent Deadpool film.

Creating "**Deadpool**" (2016) was not just an issue of interpreting comic book boards onto the screen. Reynolds, close by chief Tim Mill operator, fastidiously molded a film that embraced the person's brand name humor as well as dove into the intricacies underneath the red spandex. The adults-only nature of the film was a takeoff from the customary superhuman passage, permitting Deadpool to break free from the imperatives of a clean story.

Reynolds, in typifying Deadpool, turned out to be more than an entertainer in an ensemble. The red spandex, katana-employing persona turned into his very own expansion flippant soul. The genuineness, the mind, and the capacity to flawlessly break the fourth wall were all components painstakingly sharpened to catch the substance of this unusual person.

Past the on-screen depiction, Reynolds turned into an indefatigable supporter of the film. Drawing in with fans via online entertainment, partaking in unusual showcasing efforts, and embracing Deadpool's special kind of humor in limited-time endeavors, he raised the person from a comic book screw-up to a social peculiarity.

The progress of "**Deadpool**" re-imagined Reynolds' professional direction as well as making a permanent imprint on the hero. The film's victory went past film industry numbers; it was a demonstration of the force of remaining consistent with the center of a person, regardless of whether that character is a contemptuous, leg-pulling screw-up like Deadpool. In becoming Deadpool, Reynolds didn't simply wear the ensemble; he reinvigorated a person who challenged shows and turned into an image of imaginative valor in Hollywood.

CHAPTER 6

Producer and Entrepreneur

Ryan Reynolds' endeavor into the domains of Producer and business person has added a powerful layer to his complex profession, exhibiting a business sharpness that stretches out past the spotlight of Hollywood.

In his job as a Producer, Reynolds has effectively formed projects that line up with his imaginative vision. One outstanding endeavor is the film **"Deadpool"** (2016), where he featured as the protagonist as well as assumed an essential part in shepherding the film through its different stages. His inclusion went past the limits of a conventional driving entertainer, as he worked together with the imaginative group to guarantee the film caught the flippant pitch of the notorious wannabe. The outcome of **"Deadpool"** cemented Reynolds' situation in Hollywood as well as denoted a victory for his ability as a maker with a particular imaginative vision.

Reynolds' enterprising soul tracked down articulation in the business world, most eminently with his possession stake in Avionics American Gin. His entrance into the spirits business was not a simple superstar support but rather a key and active contribution to the brand. Reynolds utilized his image and participated in creative promoting procedures, transforming Aviation Gin into a significant player in the serious spirits market. His capacity to rise above the customary limits of superstar support and effectively add to the development of the brand embodies his enterprising methodology.

Past the spirits business, Reynolds has investigated different pioneering adventures, utilizing his notoriety and business experiences. His readiness to broaden past the bounds of acting mirrors an essential mentality and a craving to leave an enduring effect past the screen.

In the crossing point of maker and business person, Reynolds has shown an ability to explore the imaginative and business scenes with equivalent artfulness. The collaboration between his imaginative undertakings in Hollywood and his enterprising endeavors highlights an all-encompassing way to deal with his vocation, where every feature supplements the other. Reynolds' introduction to creation and business venture fills in as a moving illustration of a Hollywood figure embracing the job of an entertainer as well as an essential player in forming the stories both on and off the screen.

Aviation Gin and Other Ventures

Ryan Reynolds' introduction to the business world has been set apart by remarkable endeavors, with Aviation American Gin remaining a lead illustration of his innovative achievement.

★ Aeronautics American Gin

Reynolds' proprietorship stake in Aviation American Gin goes past a commonplace VIP support. His contribution involves an essential methodology that has changed the brand into a central part of the cutthroat spirits industry. Reynolds, as opposed to being a simple face for the brand, effectively takes part in showcasing efforts, mixes his contemptuous humor into limited-time endeavors, and takes part in molding the brand's personality. This degree of possession and responsibility has added to the gin's business accomplishment as well as raised Reynolds into the position of superstar business visionary having an enduring effect on their endeavors.

★ Different Endeavors

Reynolds' enterprising soul reaches out past the spirits business. Enhancement is a vital topic in his undertakings, exhibiting an essential methodology that lines up with his image and interests. While explicit insights concerning different endeavors might fluctuate, Reynolds has investigated a scope of pioneering tries that influenced his fame and business experiences. This eagerness to investigate different business valuable open doors mirrors a smart commitment to enterprises that reverberates with the two his persona and more extensive market patterns.

Ryan Reynolds' endeavors, especially Aviation American Gin, typify his job as a functioning and key player in the business world. His prosperity isn't simply monetary yet additionally originates from a veritable and involved obligation to the brands he connects with. This enterprising excursion grandstands Reynolds' capacity to explore and impact ventures past the marvelousness of Hollywood, leaving an enduring engraving as a big-name business person with a particular and effective presence in the business domain.

CHAPTER 7

<u>Challenges and Triumphs</u>

Ryan Reynolds' excursion in media outlets has been an embroidery woven with the two difficulties and wins, reflecting the eccentric idea of Hollywood as well as his flexibility and capacity to explore the intricacies of a unique profession.

➤ Challenges

1. Early Vocation Battles: In the same way as other entertainers, Reynolds confronted difficulties in the beginning phases of his profession. Beginning undertakings, including TV jobs and early movies, were met with fluctuating levels of progress, and advancement minutes were tricky.

2. Exploring Pigeonholing: Reynolds needed to explore the test of being pigeonholed in specific jobs right off the bat in his profession. Defeating the impression of

being a particular sort of entertainer expected key decisions and a guarantee to exhibiting his flexibility.

3. Film industry Misfortunes: Only one out of every odd venture appreciated business achievement, and Reynolds experienced mishaps in the cinema world. Films like "**Green Lantern**" confronted blended audits and didn't make the normal progress, adding to the recurring pattern of his Hollywood direction.

➢ Triumphs

1. Leap forward with "**Deadpool**": The delegated win in Reynolds' profession accompanied "**Deadpool**" (2016). The film not only broke film industry records for an adults-only film but also re-imagined the superhuman classification. Reynolds' devotion to the undertaking, both as an entertainer and maker, denoted a defining moment in his vocation.

2. Flexibility in Jobs: Reynolds won over pigeonholing by exhibiting his adaptability in different jobs. His capacity to flawlessly change between classifications,

from rom-coms to activity-stuffed superhuman movies, exhibited his reach as an entertainer.

3. Accomplishment as a Producer: The progress of **"Deadpool"** slung Reynolds into the domain of fruitful makers. His contribution in molding the task, combined with his imaginative vision, displayed another element of his vocation past acting.

4. Innovative Endeavors: Reynolds' endeavors past Hollywood, especially his responsibility for American Gin, exhibited his ability as a business visionary. The progress of these endeavors added a layer of achievement past the conventional markers of a Hollywood profession.

5. Online Entertainment Presence: Reynolds' clever and drawing presence via web-based entertainment has turned into a victory in the computerized domain. His capacity to interface with fans through humor, legitimate collaborations, and shrewd showcasing further sets his status as a darling figure in mainstream society.

Ryan Reynolds' process is a demonstration of the repeating idea of media outlets, where difficulties are met with strength, prompting wins that rethink vocations. From defeating pigeonholing to making extraordinary progress with **"Deadpool"** and broadening his impact into the business world, Reynolds' story is one of development, versatility, and win notwithstanding misfortune.

Career Ups and Downs

Ryan Reynolds' Hollywood process has been a rollercoaster ride, set apart by snapshots of wins and difficulties that formed the direction of his profession.

➤ Ups

1. Leap forward with "**Van Wilder**": Reynolds earned broad respect for his job in "**Van Wilder: Party Liaison**" (2002). The film turned into a clique exemplary, exhibiting Reynolds' comedic ability and making way for more extensive open doors in the business.

2. Basic Recognition in "**Buried**": Reynolds got basic praise for his presentation in the thrill ride "**Buried**" (2010), where the whole film unfurls with him covered alive. The job showed his capacity to convey a film with serious and sensational subjects.

3. Accomplishment with "**Deadpool**": The apex of Reynolds' profession accompanied "**Deadpool**" (2016). The film not only broke film industry records for an

adult-only film but also reclassified the hero class. Reynolds' devotion to the undertaking, both as an entertainer and maker, denoted a defining moment in his vocation.

4. Adaptability in Sports: Reynolds exhibited flexibility by effectively exploring different sorts. From rom-coms like "**The Proposal**" (2009) to activity-stuffed superhuman jobs in "**Deadpool**" and "**Deadpool 2**" (2018), he exhibited a reach that resonated with different crowds.

5. Wandering into Creation and Business: Reynolds wandered into creation with projects like "**Deadpool**" and embraced business ventures with the responsibility for American Gin. These endeavors displayed his business insight as well as added new aspects to his profession past acting.

➢ Downs

1. Early Profession Battles: Reynolds confronted difficulties in the beginning phases of his profession, with a few TV jobs and movies not building up

forward movement. These early battles were a typical involvement with Hollywood however added to the vulnerabilities of a maturing entertainer.

2. Film industry Misfortunes: Only one out of every odd undertaking made business progress. Films like **"Green Lantern"** (2011) confronted blended audits and film industry disillusionments, adding to the unavoidable ebbs in Reynolds' Hollywood direction.

3. Pigeonholing Difficulties: Reynolds experienced difficulties related to being pigeonholed from the get-go in his profession. Conquering the impression of being restricted to explicit jobs expected key decisions and a promise to display his flexibility.

Generally, Ryan Reynolds' profession has been a unique exchange of ups and downs. While confronting difficulties and difficulties, he has reliably bounced back with triumphs that rethink his status in Hollywood. From leading-edge jobs to adventures past acting, Reynolds' professional process is a demonstration of versatility, flexibility, and the erratic idea of media outlets.

Overcoming Setbacks and Embracing Success

Ryan Reynolds' excursion in media outlets typifies the account of versatility, where mishaps are not hindrances but rather venturing stones to possible victory. His capacity to explore difficulties and embrace achievement has shaped a story that goes past the traditional ups and downs of Hollywood.

➢ Setbacks

1. Early Vocation Difficulties: Reynolds confronted the obstacles run by the mill of yearning entertainers. Early TV jobs and film projects didn't necessarily convert into moment achievements. This stage tried his purpose and gave the essential encounters that would later add to his development.

2. Film industry Frustrations: Despite early victories, few out of every odd undertaking accomplished the ideal business recognition. Films like "**Green Lantern**" (2011) confronted blended audits and film industry mishaps, featuring the eccentric idea of the business.

3. Pigeonholing Concerns: Reynolds wrestled with the test of being pigeonholed in unambiguous jobs. Breaking liberated from these assumptions expected vital decisions and conscious work to feature his flexibility past specific person originals.

➤ Beating Mishaps

1. Enhancing Jobs: Reynolds explored the test of pigeonholing by deliberately enhancing his jobs. Progressing from comedic exhibitions in films like "**Van Wilder**" to sensational jobs in projects like "**Buried**," he displayed a reach that overcame early presumption.

2. Vital Profession Decisions: Gaining from difficulties, Reynolds settled on essential professional decisions that suited him for progress. His contribution to projects like "**Deadpool**" displayed his acting ability as well as denoted a shift into delivering, giving him imaginative control and impact.

3. Versatility and Flexibility: Reynolds' versatility despite misfortunes mirrors a capacity to adjust to the advancing scene of the business. Instead of being

prevented by dissatisfaction, he diverted these encounters into fuel for development and improvement.

➤ Embracing Achievement

1. Forward leap with "**Deadpool**": The defining moment in Reynolds' profession accompanied "**Deadpool**" (2016). The film re-imagined the superhuman type as well as set Reynolds' status as a main entertainer and maker. The outcome of "**Deadpool**" displayed his devotion and innovative vision.

2. Adaptability in Types: Reynolds' prosperity isn't bound to a particular classification. His capacity to flawlessly change between comedic jobs, activity-stuffed superhuman movies, and extreme dramatizations highlights his flexibility and interest in assorted crowds.

3. Wandering Past Acting: Reynolds embraced achievement through going about as well as by wandering into creation and business. His responsibility for American Gin and other business tries

added layers to his vocation, exhibiting an all-encompassing methodology past the bounds of acting.

4. Computerized Commitment and Individual Brand: Reynolds' clever drawing in presence via virtual entertainment stages added to his prosperity. His true cooperation, cunning showcasing, and funny substance charmed him to fans as well as hardened his image in the advanced age.

Ryan Reynolds' process is a story of beating difficulties through strength, vital decisions, and flexibility. His professional direction represents that achievement is not a straight path but a unique exchange of difficulties, development, and the faithful obligation to develop as a craftsman and business person. Reynolds' story is a demonstration of the extraordinary force of persistence in the steadily developing scene of media outlets.

CHAPTER 8

<u>Charity and Advocacy</u>

Ryan Reynolds' obligation to good cause and support mirrors a profound awareness of certain expectations past the fabulousness of Hollywood, displaying a certified commitment to having a constructive outcome on the world.

★ Altruistic Drives

Reynolds has been effectively associated with a few generous undertakings, adding to causes that line up with his qualities and a longing to impact significant change. His altruistic endeavors reach out to past monetary commitments, frequently including involved commitment and bringing issues to light for different issues.

★ Psychological Wellness Promotion

One of the things that makes Reynolds' heart is emotional well-being promotion. He has been a straightforward ally, utilizing his foundation to destigmatize emotional wellness issues and advance open discussions. Reynolds has shared individual encounters, underlining the significance of looking for help and encouraging a caring comprehension of emotional wellness challenges.

★ Youngsters' Wellbeing and Prosperity

Reynolds has shown a critical obligation to work on the existence of youngsters. His inclusion with associations zeroed in on youngsters' well-being and prosperity highlights a commitment to making a positive effect on the more youthful age. Whether through gathering pledges or direct commitment, Reynolds tries to add to a more promising time to come for youngsters confronting wellbeing challenges.

★ Support for Natural Causes

Ecological backing is another region where Reynolds has coordinated his endeavors. His obligation to manageability and natural protection lines up with a more extensive consciousness of worldwide issues. Reynolds effectively upholds drives pointed toward tending to environmental change, advancing eco-accommodating practices, and defending the planet for people in the future.

★ Catastrophe Alleviation

Reynolds has rushed to answer helpful emergencies, adding to catastrophe aid projects all over the planet. Whether through monetary guidance, raising money missions, or utilizing his impact to energize support, Reynolds has reliably exhibited a pledge to give help with the outcome of cataclysmic events and crises.

★ Political and Social Issues

Past unambiguous causes, Reynolds has utilized his foundation to advocate for social and policy-centered issues. His commitment to conversations encompassing balance, common liberties, and metro commitment mirrors a more extensive obligation to being a socially cognizant figure. Reynolds doesn't avoid resolving significant cultural issues, taking advantage of his leverage to enhance voices and advance positive change.

★ Individual Contribution and Effect

What recognizes Reynolds' way of dealing with noble causes and backing is his contribution. Past being a nonentity, he effectively draws in with the causes he upholds. Whether taking part in occasions, starting efforts, or utilizing his virtual entertainment presence to bring issues to light, Reynolds guarantees that his commitments go past money-related help, having an unmistakable effect through involved contribution.

Ryan Reynolds' obligation to noble cause and support goes past the job of a superstar figure composing a check. It embodies a real enthusiasm for having an effect, an eagerness to capitalize on his leverage for positive change, and confidence in the groundbreaking force of aggregate endeavors to resolve major problems confronting society. Reynolds' magnanimous undertakings act as a rousing instance of involving notoriety as a power for good, where each beneficent demonstration adds to a more extensive story of empathy, mindfulness, and positive change.

Causes Close to His Heart

Ryan Reynolds has supported a different scope of causes, mirroring a charitable portfolio that lines up with his qualities and a profound obligation to have a beneficial outcome for society. The Makes Close His Heart features a comprehensive way to deal with charity, resolving issues going from psychological well-being to natural protection.

★ Emotional Wellness Promotion

One of the causes that Reynolds holds near his heart is emotional wellness mindfulness. Drawing from individual encounters, he has turned into a noticeable supporter for breaking the shame-encompassing psychological well-being issues. Reynolds effectively participates in discussions, shares his battles, and advances getting it and compassion. His point isn't just to destigmatize psychological well-being but additionally to energize open discourse and emotionally supportive networks for those confronting difficulties.

★ Youngsters' Wellbeing and Prosperity

Reynolds has shown a significant obligation to work on the existence of kids. He effectively upholds associations devoted to kids' well-being and prosperity, partaking in drives that give assets and help to young people confronting well-being challenges. Reynolds' association goes past monetary commitments, frequently including individual visits to pediatric clinics and dynamic cooperation in occasions that elevate and uphold kids.

★ Ecological Preservation

Natural causes are one more key concentration for Reynolds. He advocates for maintainability, and preservation, and endeavors to battle environmental change. Perceiving the pressing need to resolve ecological issues, Reynolds upholds drives that advance eco-accommodating practices, safeguard normal territories, and add to a more manageable future. His responsibility mirrors a more extensive familiarity with the interconnectedness between natural well-being and generally speaking prosperity.

★ **Calamity Alleviation**

Amid philanthropic emergencies and catastrophic events, Reynolds has been an unfaltering ally of calamity aid ventures. He guides assets and utilizes his foundation to assemble support, empowering others to add to alleviation drives. Reynolds' obligation to catastrophe helps highlight an acknowledgment of the quick and dire requirements of networks confronting misfortune.

★ **Social and Political Support**

Reynolds effectively participates in upholding social and political causes. Whether it's advancing equity, common freedoms, or city commitment, he takes advantage of his leverage to enhance voices and drive positive change. Reynolds conforms to drives that intend to make a more comprehensive and just society, exhibiting a promise to resolve foundational issues and support a superior future.

The close Ryan Reynolds' heart epitomizes a range of cultural worries, from psychological wellness and kids' prosperity to natural preservation and civil rights. His charitable endeavors stretch out past monetary commitments, integrating individual commitment, backing, and a certifiable longing to make an enduring and significant effect on the world. Reynolds' obligation to these causes mirrors a comprehensive way to deal with charity, where every drive adds to a more extensive story of positive change and social improvement.

CHAPTER 9

Legacy in Hollywood

Ryan Reynolds' heritage in Hollywood is a multi-layered embroidery woven with flexibility, versatility, and a groundbreaking effect on media outlets. Past the regular markers of fame, Reynolds has made a permanent imprint that reaches out from his critical exhibitions to his endeavors underway, business, and altruism.

★ Adaptability as an Entertainer

Reynolds' heritage as an entertainer is characterized by his noteworthy flexibility. From early comedic jobs in films like "**Van Wilder**" to the extraordinary and sensational exhibition in "**Buried**," he has displayed a reach that rises above sort limits. His capacity to flawlessly progress between types, including rom-coms, activity-pressed hero movies and provocative dramatizations, separates him as an entertainer equipped for epitomizing different characters.

★ Social Contact with "Deadpool"

The pinnacle of Reynolds' heritage lies in his depiction of Deadpool in the eponymous movie. " **Deadpool**" (2016) and its spin-off denoted a change in perspective in the superhuman classification, breaking customary standards with its adults-only methodology and flippant humor. Reynolds rejuvenated the notable wannabe as well as assumed a vital part in delivering and molding the story. The outcome of "**Deadpool**" turned into a social peculiarity, engraving Reynolds as a key figure who reclassified the assumptions for superhuman movies.

★ Maker and Pioneering Adventures

Reynolds' introduction to creation is a demonstration of his craving to shape stories both before and behind the camera. His association with projects like "**Deadpool**" exhibited his acting ability as well as his capacity to explore the imaginative parts of filmmaking.

Past Hollywood, Reynolds' innovative endeavors, especially with Aviation American Gin, added a business aspect to his inheritance. His outcome in the spirits business and other pioneering tries highlights a comprehensive way to deal with his vocation, reaching out past customary acting jobs.

★ Magnanimity and Social Effect

The magnanimous undertakings near Reynolds' heart contribute essentially to his heritage. His promotion of psychological wellness, support for youngsters' prosperity, obligation to natural causes, and commitment to calamity help mirror a profound feeling of social obligation. Reynolds utilizes his leverage to intensify voices on cultural issues, leaving a heritage that reaches out past the screen and into the more extensive domains of positive social effect.

★ Advanced Presence and Commitment

Reynolds' heritage isn't bound to conventional mediums; it stretches out into the computerized scene. His clever and drawing presence via virtual entertainment stages has made a special association with fans. Reynolds uses these stages for self-advancement as well as to share humor, participate in bona fide collaborations, and add to a computerized culture that rises above the limits of customary superstar personas.

All in all, Ryan Reynolds' heritage in Hollywood is a rich story woven with imagination, versatility, and a promise to have a significant effect. His flexibility as an entertainer, extraordinary job in reclassifying the hero classification, wanders into creation and business ventures, charitable undertakings, and connecting with computerized presence, all in all, shape a heritage that goes past the limits of a regular Hollywood profession. Reynolds remains a figure whose impact reaches out into different circles, making a getting-through imprint on media outlets and then some.

Impact on the Film Industry

Ryan Reynolds fundamentally affects the entertainment world in more ways than one:

★ Film industry Achievement

Reynolds has featured in various film industry hits, including "**Deadpool**" (2016), which earned more than $783 million around the world, and "**Free Guy**" (2021), which netted more than $331 million around the world. These triumphs have exhibited his capacity to draw crowds and produce income for studios.

★ Type Development

Reynolds has effectively explored different classifications, from activity comedies like "**Deadpool**" to rom-coms like "**The Proposal**" (2009) and dramatizations like "**Buried**" (2010). This flexibility has permitted him to interface with many crowds and secure himself as a main entertainer in Hollywood.

Mindfulness and Humor: Reynolds is known for his humble humor and ability to embrace his on-screen personas. This has charmed him to fans and made him a well-known figure in the business. His promoting lobbies for films like "**Deadpool**" have been especially lauded for their mind and inventiveness.

★ Creation and Business venture

Reynolds has extended his association in the business past acting. He helped to establish Greatest Exertion, a showcasing and media organization that has delivered films like "**Deadpool**" and "**Free Guy**." He likewise claims Aviation American Gin and has put resources into different organizations.

★ Brand Associations

Reynolds' fame and promoting shrewdness have made him a pursued brand accomplice. He has worked with organizations like Aviation Gin, Mint Portable, and Matchbox to make effective advertising efforts that have additionally improved his image offer.

★ Web-based Entertainment Impact

Reynolds is perhaps one of the most compelling entertainers via web-based entertainment, with more than 40 million devotees on Instagram. He utilizes his foundation to draw in fans, advance his activities, and back different causes.

★ Industry Regard

Reynolds is broadly regarded in the entertainment world for his ability, hard-working attitude, and business astuteness. He has been assigned various honors and has procured the esteem of his companions and associates.

★ Crowd Allure

Reynolds' mystique, humor, and interesting persona have made him a famous figure among crowds around the world. He has areas of strength for a base that enthusiastically follows his work and supports his undertakings.

★ Influence on Superhuman Kind

Reynolds' depiction of Deadpool is generally viewed as one of the most famous and fruitful superhuman exhibitions lately. His contemptuous, mindful way of dealing with the person has re-imagined the class and roused different studios to face more innovative challenges.

★ Future Potential

Reynolds is still somewhat youthful and can keep having a tremendous effect on the entertainment world for a long time to come. His ability, flexibility, and business sharpness propose that he has a long and effective profession in front of him.

Future Projects and Aspirations

Ryan Reynolds is an exceptionally effective entertainer, maker, and business visionary with a brilliant future in front of him. He has a demonstrated history of progress in both film and TV, and he is continually expanding his points of view with new undertakings and adventures.

Here are some of Ryan Reynolds' future ventures and goals:

★ **Kept Acting Achievement**

Reynolds is currently in his prime as an entertainer, and he makes certain to keep featuring in significant blockbusters in the years to come. He has a few ventures being developed, including a spin-off of the widely praised film "**The Adam Project**" and a likely third portion in the "**Deadpool**" establishment.

★ **Producer Greatness**

Reynolds has likewise set up a good foundation for himself as a fruitful maker, and he is probably going to keep creating films under his Greatest Exertion pennant. He has a skill for distinguishing and creating promising ventures, and he has a demonstrated history of conveying excellent diversion.

★ Enterprising Endeavors

Reynolds is a keen financial specialist, and he makes certain to keep growing his pioneering portfolio in the years to come. He has previously put resources into a few effective organizations, and he is continuously searching for new chances to develop his domain.

★ Magnanimous Undertakings

Reynolds is likewise an enthusiastic donor, and he is focused on utilizing his foundation to help significant causes. He is a vocal promoter of psychological wellness mindfulness, and he has worked with a few associations to fund-raise and mindfulness for emotional well-being issues.

★ Future Desires

In the long haul, Reynolds wants to change into coordinating and composing. He has an imaginative vision that he might want to impart to the world, and he accepts that guiding and composing would permit him to have more command over his inventive strategy.

By and large, Ryan Reynolds is a multi-layered ability with a brilliant future in front of him. He makes certain to keep having a huge effect on the entertainment world and then some, and he is a motivation yearning for entertainers, makers, and business visionaries all over.

CHAPTER 10

<u>Reflecting on a Remarkable Career</u>

Ryan Reynolds is a Canadian-American entertainer, maker, and businessperson who has had a surprising vocation in the entertainment world. He has featured in various fruitful movies, including "**Deadpool**" (2016), "**Free Guy**" (2021), and "**The Adam Project**" (2022). He is likewise an effective maker and business person, and he is known for his humble humor and showcasing canny.

➤ Early Vocation

Ryan Reynolds started his vocation during the 1990s with jobs in network shows, for example, "**Hillside**" (1991-1993) and "**Two Guys and a Girl**" (1998-2001). He made his film debut in 1993 with the Canadian film.

➢ Advancement Jobs

Reynolds' leading-edge job came in 2002 with the satire film "**National Lampoon's Van Wilder**". He followed this up with jobs in movies, for example, "**Blade: Trinity**" (2004), "**Waiting**..." (2005), and "**Just Friends**" (2005).

➢ Lighthearted comedy Star

In the last part of the 2000s, Reynolds turned into a main man in lighthearted comedies. He featured in movies, for example, "**Definitely, Maybe**" (2008), "**The Proposal**" (2009), and "**Self/Less**" (2015).

➢ Activity Star

During the 2010s, Reynolds started to make more move jobs. He featured in movies, for example, "**Green lantern**" (2011), "**R.I.P.D.**" (2013), and "**6 Underground**" (2019).

➢ Deadpool

Reynolds' most famous job is without a doubt Deadpool. He originally played the person in the 2016 film of a similar name. He repeated the job for the spin-off, "**Deadpool 2**" (2018).

➢ Maker and Business Visionary

Reynolds is likewise an effective maker and business visionary. He helped to establish Most Extreme Exertion, a promoting and media organization that has delivered movies, for example, "**Deadpool**" and "**Free Guy**". He additionally claims Aviation American Gin and has put resources into different organizations.

➢ Influence on the Entertainment world

Ryan Reynolds essentially affects the entertainment world. He is a flexible entertainer who has featured in a large number of fruitful movies. He is likewise an insightful maker and business visionary. Reynolds is known for his humble humor and showcasing wisdom, and he has turned into a famous figure in the business.

CONCLUSION

The pages of this book have unfurled the spellbinding story of Ryan Reynolds — an entertainer, maker, businessperson, and giver whose excursion rises above the glamor of Hollywood. From the early moves that formed his versatility to the victories that reclassified classifications, Reynolds has impressed by being a multi-layered force in media outlets.

His inheritance isn't bound to the cinema; it reaches out into the domains of creation and business venture, where Reynolds' innovative vision has made a permanent imprint. The contemptuous and momentous depiction of Deadpool remains a social achievement, highlighting his extraordinary effect on the hero type.

Reynolds' endeavors past Hollywood, especially in the business world and generosity, grandstand a pledge to genuineness and positive social effect. His humanitarian undertakings, tending to emotional wellness, kids' prosperity, and natural preservation, mirror a profound feeling of social obligation.

As the last part unfurls, it uncovers an inheritance that goes past regular limits, formed by strength, flexibility, and a steady commitment to having a significant effect. Ryan Reynolds arises as a Hollywood star as well as an image of imaginative bravery, an essential business person, and a giver whose impact stretches out a long way past the edges of a film reel.

In the parts of Reynolds' life, we find a story that rouses, engages, and reverberates with the powerful soul of a complex person. As the book closes, the persevering tradition of Ryan Reynolds is a demonstration of the extraordinary force of embracing difficulties, rethinking standards, and leaving a positive engraving on the world — one realistic second, one innovative endeavor, and each generous demonstration in turn.

Manufactured by Amazon.ca
Acheson, AB

32238843R00050